sweet*blessings*
FROM OUR HOME

Merry Christmas
2007
Love, Janet

ELIZABETH O. STEEDLEY

sweet*blessings*
FROM OUR HOME

TATE PUBLISHING & *Enterprises*

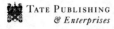

TATE PUBLISHING
& Enterprises

Tate Publishing is committed to excellence in the publishing industry. Our staff of highly trained professionals, including editors, graphic designers, and marketing personnel, work together to produce the very finest books available. The company reflects the philosophy established by the founders, based on Psalms 68:11,

"THE LORD GAVE THE WORD AND GREAT WAS THE COMPANY OF
THOSE WHO PUBLISHED IT."

If you would like further information, please contact us:
1.888.361.9473 | www.tatepublishing.com
TATE PUBLISHING & Enterprises, LLC | 127°. Trade Center Terrace
Mustang, Oklahoma 73064 USA

This title is also available as a Tate Out Loud product.
Visit www.tatepublishing.com for more information

Published in the United States of America

ISBN: 978-1-5988691-7-X

07.03.20

This book is dedicated to
my Lord and Savior, Jesus Christ.
without Him, I would be nothing.

To my precious husband Jody:
you are my rock. I love you.

To Laci, Heyward, Lindsey Kate and Micajah:
thank you for showing me what matters in life.

To my Mom for instilling in me a love for cooking
and for teaching me how.

To my friends and family that contributed to this cookbook:
thank you for the Sweet Blessings you are.

table of contents

foreword

*I*t is a wonderful thing to grow up with someone who has a gift for cooking. My sister Elizabeth always, even as a small child, had a desire and a talent for preparing food. Many of us, myself included, are capable of following a recipe, and by that I mean combining ingredients in the right proportions (lets say most of us are *usually* capable of this). However, being able to successfully combine ingredients is quite a different thing from understanding how ingredients work together to create unique flavors, textures and tastes. To Elizabeth this has always come naturally.

We have many good cooks in our family, and growing up we spent a great deal of time cooking with our mother, aunts and grandmothers. As we got older, we loved nothing more than to make breakfast for all of our friends before school, or prepare special dinners for our own family. Only later did I realize that not everyone learns how to cook growing up; that many people become adults without mastering more than a microwave (but that will have to be covered in another book, Lizzie). I didn't realize that learning to cook can be such an asset.

This volume of recipes reveals a person with a passion for food, someone who still enjoys sharing her talent, someone who *never fails* to gather friends and family together for special occasions, to bless them with a spirit of graciousness and a wonderful meal.

Katharine Owens
Enschede, Netherlands, 2006

appetizers & beverages

cheddar pennies

Ingredients

½ cup butter

½ pound grated cheddar cheese

¼ teaspoon salt

3 tablespoons onion soup mix

1 cup flour

. . . .

Mix all ingredients with electric mixer until well blended. Shape into two sausage shaped rolls and freeze. Slice thin and bake at 375° in pre-heated oven for 10 minutes

artichoke dip

3 jars artichoke hearts, drained well

1 cup mayonnaise

1 cup grated Parmesan cheese

. . . .

Mix ingredients in food processor, pulsing to not mix too finely.
Pour into casserole dish and bake at 350° for 30 minutes, until bubbly.
Serve warm with Buttery crackers.

vidalia onion dip

Ingredients

3 cups chopped Vidalia onion

3 cups Swiss cheese, grated

2 cups mayonnaise

1 teaspoon garlic powder or salt

• • • • • • • • • • • • • • • • • • • •

Combine all ingredients and pour into a pan sprayed with cooking oil.

Bake at 350° for about 23–30 minutes until bubbly.

Serve hot with butter crackers.

cocktail weenies

Ingredients

1 jar grape jelly

1 jar BBQ sauce

1 package cocktail weenies

. . . .

Combine and simmer on stove or simmer in a crock pot until hot.

*As an alternative, you may use Ketchup instead of BBQ sauce.

easy mexican dip

My friends Kalynn McLaine and Shelley Dye introduced this easy dip to us. It is delicious and so easy!

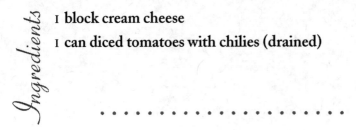

Ingredients

1 **block cream cheese**

1 **can diced tomatoes with chilies (drained)**

. . . .

*M*ix in microwave safe bowl and heat for about 1 minute or until softened. Stir and serve with tortilla chips.

*Salsa can be substituted for diced tomatoes for a different flavor.

taco dip

Ingredients

1 block of cream cheese (8 oz)
1 can chili (without beans)
1 cup grated cheddar cheese
black olives, tomatoes, peppers
Tortilla Chips

. . . .

Soften cream cheese in 9 x 13 baking dish in 350° oven. Remove from oven and spread in pan with spatula. Spread chili over cream cheese. Top with grated cheese. Top with other toppings such as black olives, tomatoes and peppers. Return to oven and bake until cheese is melted (approximately 10 minutes). Serve with chips.

layered nacho dip

1 can (16 oz) refried beans

½ package Taco seasoning mix

1 (6 oz) carton Avocado dip

1 (8 oz) carton sour cream

1 (4 ½ oz) can chopped black olives

2 large tomatoes, diced

1 package shredded Monterey Jack Cheese

. . . .

Layer in above order and serve with nacho chips.

guacamole

My brother-in-law Mike is an excellent cook. Usually when they come home to visit, they stay with my mom, so I don't get to sample much of his cooking. Last time they were home, he made this guacamole and I called as soon as they got home to find out how to make it!

Ingredients

2 ripe avocados

1 ½ tablespoons sour cream

Juice of ½ lemon (or a whole lime)

small red onion, finely chopped

fresh chopped cilantro

1 teaspoon cumin powder

Salt and Pepper

. . . .

Slice avocados lengthwise in half and remove from skin with spoon or spatula. Put in medium sized bowl and add other ingredients.

Use fork to mash together to smooth consistency.

Add salt and pepper to taste.

swamp salsa

My friend, Jenny Robbins, introduced this salsa to me. After tasting it at her house, I immediately went to the store to pick up the ingredients to make some at home. I then called my mom and told her to go to the store; she was going to have to try this! The ingredients sound a little strange, but it is SO delicious!

Ingredients

1 can black beans
1 can white shoe peg corn
1 large can crushed pineapple
1 can diced tomatoes with chili peppers
1 small bottle Italian Dressing

. . . .

Pour black beans, corn, pineapple and tomatoes in a colander. Rinse and drain. Pour into large bowl and add dressing.
Serve with Taco chips.

cream cheese & olive rolls

This recipe comes from my good friend Amanda James.

Ingredients

1 8 oz block of cream cheese
1 small can chopped black olives
one package Flour tortillas

. . . .

Mix cream cheese and olives. Spread onto tortillas and roll up.
Then slice making circular pieces. Serve with salsa for dipping.
*My friend Susie Brown makes these, but mixes salsa with the cream
cheese & olives instead of for dipping.

toasted pecans

Ingredients

3 tablespoons melted butter
1 pound pecan halves
1 tablespoon salt

. . . .

*M*ix melted butter and pecans. Sprinkle with salt and stir until evenly coated. Pour into shallow baking dish and bake at 200° for about an hour stirring every 15 minutes.

sweet and salty nuts

This delicious recipe is from my mother-in-law, Elizabeth Steedley.
Be careful, these are addictive!

Ingredients

1 lb walnut pieces or pecan halves (4 ½ cups)
½ cup granulated sugar
1/3 cup white corn syrup
coarse sea salt or kosher salt
(1 tablespoon or 2 teaspoons salt)
½ teaspoon fresh ground black pepper
coarse raw sugar
2 tablespoons Butter

. . . .

Butter baking pan. In a large bowl, stir nuts, granulated sugar, corn
syrup, salt and pepper, spread in pan. Bake for 25 minutes or until
golden brown, stirring once or twice. Remove from oven, sprinkle with
raw sugar, toss to coat. Transfer to foil, cool then break apart.

hot crab dip

This is a low fat recipe and oh, so good!

Ingredients

½ cup skim milk

1/3 cup salsa

3 packages (8 oz) light cream cheese, cubed

2 packages (8 oz each) imitation crab meat, flaked

1 cup thinly sliced green onions.

. . . .

Combine milk and salsa. Transfer to crockpot sprayed with cooking spray. Stir in other ingredients. Cover and cook on low for 3–4 hours stirring every 30 minutes. Serve hot with Melba Toast or crackers.

shrimp spread

Ingredients

3 cans medium shrimp

1 oz package of cream cheese

add to taste:

lots of lemon juice

mayonnaise

onion juice

Worcestershire sauce

. . . .

Blend all ingredients in a food processor and chill.

Serve with crackers.

fish cakes

My brother-in-law, Mike Maier, introduced us to these. They are a twist on the traditional Crab Cakes.

Ingredients

4 Tilapia Filets (or any firm white fish)
1 cup (about 20 medium sized) shrimp; peeled, heads off and de-veined
1 ½ cups fresh bread crumbs
2 eggs
salt and pepper
2 teaspoons curry powder
Fresh herbs (one or any combination of basil, cilantro or dill)

. . . .

With food processor, make fresh breadcrumbs first (best is stale white bread). Put 1 cup in large mixing bowl. Roughly chop the shrimp in the food processor and add. Wash herbs thoroughly and roughly chop in food processor with filets cut into big pieces. The machine works better than hand chopping because it gives everything a ground consistency that makes it easier to form patties. Add fish mixture to bowl; add eggs, curry powder, salt and pepper. Mix well by hand. Add more bread crumbs until dry enough to make patties. Allow patties to cool in refrigerator for at least an hour. Fry in oil in non stick skillet or pan.

Makes 4–6 patties.

ham and onion
cheese ball

This recipe compliments of my friend Landa Hart. It is hard to believe it is this easy!

Ingredients

1 block cream cheese

1/3 package of chopped ham luncheon meat

2 green onions

1 teaspoon Worcestershire Sauce

1 teaspoon garlic powder

. . . .

Chop onion and luncheon meat into small pieces. Mix with other ingredients and form a ball. Refrigerate until ready to serve. May be rolled in nuts before serving. Serve with crackers.

sausage cheese balls

My grandmother used to make these when I was a little girl. I always think of her when I make them.

Ingredients

1 pound sharp cheddar cheese, grated

1 pound sausage (uncooked)

2 cups bisquick

. . . .

*M*ix and form into marble sized balls. Bake at 275 until brown.

pineapple cheese ball

My friend, Renee Harris, made this for a Bible Study one night. I had a hard time prying myself away from it.

Ingredients

1 large can crushed pineapple
1 (8 oz) cream cheese
1 ½ cups (4 x) powdered sugar
½ cup chopped pecans

. . . .

Squeeze all of the juice from the pineapple and thoroughly dry (if not, it will be sticky). Mix with cream cheese and powdered sugar. Roll in pecans before serving. Serve with cinnamon graham crackers.

chocolate cheese ball

My girlfriends and I get together once a month to play Bunco. My friend Liane Register made this when she hosted and it was SO delicious.

Ingredients

8 ounces package cream cheese, softened

½ cup butter, softened (no substitutes)

¾ cup confectioners' sugar

2 tablespoons brown sugar

¼ teaspoon vanilla extract

¾ cup miniature semi-sweet chocolate chips

¾ cup finely chopped pecans

. . . .

In a medium bowl, beat together cream cheese and butter until smooth. Mix in confectioners' sugar, brown sugar and vanilla. Stir in chocolate chips. Cover, and chill in the refrigerator for 2 hours. Shape chilled cream cheese mixture into a ball. Wrap with plastic, and chill in the refrigerator for 1 hour. Roll the cheese ball in finely chopped pecans before serving. Serve with Chocolate graham sticks.

fruit pizza

Ingredients

1 (18 oz) package refrigerated cookie dough

1 (8 oz) package cream cheese, room temperature

1/3 cup sugar

½ teaspoon vanilla extract

Fresh blueberries, banana slices, mandarin orange sections, seedless grapes, strawberry halves, kiwi fruit (or any other fruit you want), well drained

½ cup orange, peach, or apricot preserves

1 tablespoon water

. . . .

Preheat oven to 375°. Roll cookie dough to fit an ungreased 14-inch pizza pan. Bake 12 minutes or until light brown; remove from oven and cool. Combine cream cheese, sugar and vanilla. Spread over cookie dough. Arrange fruit over cream cheese. In a small saucepan over very low heat, make a glaze by heating preserves and water. Brush glaze over fruit. Chill until ready to serve.

ranch dip

In high school, my friends and I would get together from time to time and have a group lunch. Every one would bring something and we would all share. Someone brought this dip and we've been making it ever since.

Ingredients

1 (16 oz) carton Sour Cream
1 package powdered ranch dressing.

. . . .

*M*ix and chill. Serve with chips or vegetables.

plains cheese ring

It is rumored that former First Lady Rosalyn Carter used to make this, hence the name Plains. I make this all the time for parties and it always gets raves!

Ingredients

1 pound sharp cheddar cheese, grated and softened
1 cup chopped pecans
1 cup mayonnaise
1 small onion, grated
Strawberry Preserves

. . . .

Combine all ingredients except preserves. (A food processor works well). Place in ring mold greased with mayonnaise. Chill. When ready to serve, unmold and fill center with preserves. Serve with crackers or ginger snaps.

blt bites

This recipe comes from my friend Janet Wood. They are worth the extra work. She won a blue ribbon at the Timberland Jubilee Cookoff with this recipe.

Ingredients

16 to 20 **cherry tomatoes**

1 **pound bacon cooked and crumbled**

½ cup mayonnaise

1/3 cup green onion, chopped

1 tablespoon Parmesan cheese

. . . .

Cut off tops of tomatoes and scoop out pulp using small measuring spoon. Turn upside down on paper towel to drain. Mix remaining ingredients and fill each tomato. Chill until ready to serve.

vegetable pizza

My mom used to make this when I was a little girl. It is great for parties!

Ingredients

2 cans crescent rolls

2 (8 oz) cream cheese

½ cup Mayonnaise

1 package powdered ranch dressing

1 cup (or more) shredded cheddar cheese

Your favorite vegetables:

Broccoli

Mushrooms

Black olives

Carrots

Cauliflower

Peppers

. . . .

Roll out crescent rolls onto pizza pan, pinching seams to seal. Bake at 350° until brown. Mix together cream cheese, mayo and ranch dressing. Spread over cooled crust. Top with your favorite vegetables and cheese. Serve cold.

fruit dip

1 small jar marshmallow cream
1 8 oz package of cream cheese.

. . . .

Mix in food processor until well blended. Add a dash of cherry juice for color. Serve with any fruit.

brown sugar fruit dip

Ingredients

1 stick melted butter

1 cup brown sugar

1–8 oz sour cream

. . . .

*M*elt butter and stir in brown sugar. Add sour cream and stir until blended. Serve with fresh strawberries.

hot chocolate floats

Ingredients

I cup hot water

I packet instant hot cocoa mix

½ tablespoon instant coffee

Vanilla ice cream

. . . .

Mix hot water, cocoa mix, and instant coffee in a large mug. Add one scoop of vanilla ice cream and serve. Top with cinnamon sprinkles.

southern sweet tea

In the South, most people drink sweet tea. It is best served chilled over ice. You may add fresh mint or lemon.

Ingredients

1 **cup sugar**

1 **Family Sized tea bag**

2 **cups Water**

. . . .

*P*ut water, sugar and tea bag in small saucepan. Bring to a boil. Remove from heat and allow to steep for a minute or two. Pour into quart sized pitcher and fill with ice and water until full.

Keep refrigerated.

easy party punch

½ gallon sherbet (any flavor you like)

1–2 liter bottle Ginger Ale

. . . .

*M*ix in punch bowl and serve. It is slushy and delicious!

sparkling party punch

Ingredients

1 bottle White Grape Juice

1–2 liter bottle Ginger Ale

. . . .

Chill and mix in equal parts just before serving.

Serve from punch bowl with ice ring made of grape juice.

chocolate smoothie

Ingredients

2 cups Chocolate Ice Cream

2 Bananas

½ cup milk

¼ cup Chocolate Syrup

. . . .

Blend in a blender and add ice to the 4 ½ cup level.

Blend until smooth.

breads, soups, & eggs

beer bread

Ingredients

3 cups self rising flour
3 tablespoons sugar
1 (12 oz) can beer
½ cup melted butter

. . . .

Stir flour, sugar and beer together. Pour into 9 x 5 x 3 loaf pan. Pour
melted butter over top. Bake at 350° for 45 minutes.

Yield: 1 loaf

This makes great ham sandwiches

effie's biscuits

This recipe comes from my grandmother's cook, Effie. I used to love New Years at my Grandmother's house because she would make these biscuits and put ham slices in them.

Ingredients

1 cup Self Rising Flour
1 cup grated cheddar cheese
½ cup (or more) Crisco
½ cup milk
additional flour

. . . .

Flake cheese all through flour. Add Crisco and cut with two knives or pastry blender until the size of peas. Add milk until a good stiff sticky batter is formed. Put dough on the counter and work in a good bit of flour until it feels like a biscuit. Cut into any size rounds you desire.

Place onto greased pan (touching each other is OK).

Bake at 400° approximately twenty minutes, until brown.

buttermilk biscuits

My mother-in-law, Elizabeth Steedley, makes the best biscuits. The key to making tender biscuits is not to handle them too much. These measurements are approximate. Good biscuit makers know the "feel" of a good biscuit dough.

Ingredients

¼ cup Crisco
1 ½ cups Self Rising Flour
½ cup (more or less) Buttermilk
Melted butter

. . . .

Mix Crisco and flour until well blended. Add milk until right consistency. They should be slightly sticky. Turn onto floured surface or piece of waxed paper (for easier clean up). Sprinkle lightly with flour. Pat or gently roll to approximately ¾ inch. Cut with round cutter and place on cookie sheet with sides. Bake at 450° for 10 minutes or until browned. Brush with melted butter upon removal from the oven.

sour cream muffins

Ingredients

1 **cup sour cream**

2 **sticks butter, softened**

2 **cups self rising flour**

. . . .

*M*ix softened butter, sour cream and flour with a fork. Spoon into greased muffin tins. Bake at 400° for 10 minutes.

mexican corn bread

This recipe comes from my Aunt Nancy Parrott.

Ingredients

1 **box corn bread mix**
1 **small can kernel corn with juice**
1 **jalapeno pepper**
1 **egg**

. . . .

Remove seeds from pepper and finely chop pepper. Mix cornbread mix according to package directions using corn juice finished out with milk if necessary to equal liquid called for. Stir in chopped pepper and corn. Put 2 tablespoons oil in a black iron skillet. Place into cold oven set to 400° while mixing bread so it is good and hot when batter is ready. Pour batter into hot skillet and bake 20 minutes or until brown. Flip over onto a plate and put back in turned off oven until ready to serve.

banana bread

I look forward to having over-ripened bananas just to be able to make this recipe. It is best served hot right out of the oven.

Ingredients

½ cup butter

1 cup sugar

2 eggs

3 mashed ripe bananas

2 cups all purpose flour

1 teaspoon soda

1 teaspoon salt

. . . .

Cream butter and sugar. Fold in eggs. Add mashed bananas. Beat in dry ingredients. Turn into a greased 9x5x3 inch loaf pan and let stand 20 minutes. Bake in 350° degree oven for 50 minutes.

blueberry streusel muffins

Being blessed to live in Blueberry country and have fresh blueberries in our own back yard, this recipe is a favorite for Saturday mornings during the late spring and early summer.

Ingredients

2 cups self rising flour

1 ¼ cups sugar

2 eggs, slightly beaten

1 teaspoon vanilla extract

½ cup oil

½ cup milk

1 ¾ cups whole blueberries

½ cup mashed blueberries

. . . .

Combine flour and sugar in large bowl, set aside. Combine eggs, vanilla, oil and milk. Make a well in the center of the dry ingredients and pour in liquid ingredients. Stir until well mixed. Fold in all blueberries. Stir well, approximately 1 minute. Spoon batter half full into muffin tins that have been sprayed with Pam or lined with muffin papers. Sprinkle with Streusel topping and bake at 375° for 25 minutes. Makes 2 dozen muffins.

streusel topping

Ingredients

1/3 cup sugar

¼ cup all-purpose flour

2 tablespoons softened butter or margarine.

. . . .

Combine in small bowl until crumbly. Top on muffins before baking.

cream cheese coffee cake

2–8 oz cans crescent rolls

I cup sugar

2–8 oz packages cream cheese

I egg separated

I teaspoon vanilla extract

. . . .

Spread I package of rolls in 9 x 13 baking dish. Cream ¾ cup sugar, cream cheese, egg yolk and vanilla until smooth. Spread over crescent rolls. Top with remaining layer of crescent rolls. Beat egg white until frothy and spread over rolls. Sprinkle with remaining ¼ cup sugar. Bake 350 for 30–35 minutes.

caramel coffee cake

Ingredients

½ cup butter

½ cup chopped pecans

1 cup firmly packed brown sugar

2 tablespoons water

2 (8 oz) cans crescent dinner rolls

. . . .

Melt butter in a small saucepan. Spray Bundt pan with non stick spray.
Use 2 tablespoons melted butter to coat the bottom and sides of the
Bundt pan. Sprinkle the pan with 3 tablespoons of the
chopped pecans.

Add remaining nuts, brown sugar and water to remaining melted
butter. Heat to a boil, stirring occasionally. Remove dinner rolls from
package and cut (unrolled) into 16 slices. Place slices in Bundt pan
separating slightly. Spoon half of the caramel nut sauce over the slices.

Repeat with remaining rolls and caramel sauce.

Bake 350° for 25–30 minutes until golden brown.

Cool slightly turn onto serving platter and slice.

cinnamon nut swirl
coffee cake

Ingredients

1 cup Sugar

1 cup Butter

2 eggs

½ pint Sour Cream

1 teaspoon vanilla flavoring

2 cups All Purpose flour

1 teaspoon baking powder

½ teaspoon salt

1 teaspoon baking soda

½ cup nuts

1/3 cup Sugar

2 tablespoons cinnamon

. . . .

Mix nuts, sugar and cinnamon in small bowl. Set aside.

Cream butter and sugar. Beat in eggs one at a time. Add vanilla.

Sift Flour, baking powder, salt and soda and add to butter mixture.

Spread ½ of batter in greased Bundt pan. Sprinkle with ½ of nut mixture. Layer again. Run knife through slightly to swirl.

Bake at 350 for 40–50 minutes.

pancakes

Ingredients

1 cup self rising flour
1 cup milk (or buttermilk)
1 egg
1 tablespoon sugar
1 tablespoon melted butter

. . . .

Mix flour, milk and egg. Stir in sugar and melted butter.
Cook on heated skillet flipping once until brown. Serve hot!

marshmallow puffs

¼ cup sugar

1 teaspoon cinnamon

2 (8 ounce) cans crescent dinner rolls

16 large marshmallows

¼ cup melted butter

. . . .

Combine sugar and cinnamon. Separate 2 cans crescent roll dough into 16 triangles. Dip a marshmallow into melted butter and roll in cinnamon and sugar mixture. Place marshmallow on wide end of triangle. Fold corners over marshmallow and roll to the point. Pinch edges of dough to seal. Dip point side in melted butter and place butter side down in greased muffin tins. Bake at 375° 10 –15 minutes until brown. Remove from oven and drizzle with icing.

powdered sugar icing

Ingredients

½ cup confectioner's sugar

2 teaspoons milk

½ teaspoon vanilla

. . . .

Combine all ingredients and blend until smooth. Drizzle over rolls.
This icing recipe is also great for tinting and using to decorate
sugar cookies.

black bean & salsa soup

Ingredients

1 can black beans, drained and rinsed
½ jar (or more) salsa (medium hot is best)
1 can chicken broth
Sour cream
Grated Cheddar or Monterey Jack Cheese

. . . .

*P*uree beans, salsa and broth in food processor until well blended. Pour
into saucepan and heat on the stove over medium heat.
Pour into bowl and top with sour cream and Mexican cheese.

hearty chowder & potato cheese soup

The Hearty Chowder recipe comes from my dear friend Kalynn McLaine. My friend Tiffany Falgout altered it to make Potato Cheese Soup.

Ingredients

1 pound bacon

½ onion

5 white potatoes, peeled and chopped

2 carrots chopped

1 can corn

¾ teaspoon Pepper

1 teaspoon salt

4 cups water

1 pint half and half

1 ½–2 cups Velveeta

. . . .

Cook bacon and save ½ of the drippings. Sauté onion in saved drippings. Combine onions, water, potatoes, carrots and corn and cook until potatoes are tender. Add cheese and half and half. Crumble bacon and add. Do not bring to a boil again after adding half and half.

*To make Potato Cheese soup, omit carrots and corn.

white chicken chili

We love soups/chili in the winter. This is a great alternative to regular chili

Ingredients

1 package boneless/skinless chicken tenders cooked and shredded.
2 cans great northern beans, drained and rinsed
1 cans ro-tel tomatoes
2 cans chicken broth
dash of chili powder

. . . .

*M*ix all ingredients in large saucepan and simmer.
Serve with cornbread.

she crab soup

Ingredients

3 tablespoons butter

4 tablespoons flour

5 cups chicken broth

1 ½ cups heavy cream

2 cups lump crab meat

salt and white pepper to taste

½ cup sherry

. . . .

Melt butter in large saucepan. Stir in flour and cook for three minutes,
stirring constantly. Add stock and mix well with wire whisk.

Cook very slowly, uncovered, for 20 minutes.

Add cream, crabmeat, salt, pepper and sherry.

vidalia onion soup

Vidalia Onions are sweet onions that are native to Georgia. If you can't find Vidalia Onions, a sweet yellow onion will substitute.

Ingredients

6 medium Vidalia onions
¼ cup canola Oil
2 ribs celery, chopped
1 green onion, chopped
1 leek, chopped
2 Qt. chicken broth
1 cup sherry
1 cup heavy cream
2 tablespoons finely chopped fresh Thyme
Salt and White pepper

. . . .

Peel outer layer of onions and wrap onions individually in foil. Bake at
300° for 1½ hours or until tender.
Heat oil in large pot. Add green onion, leek and celery. Cook until
soft. Remove onions from foil and add to pot. Add chicken and sherry.
Simmer 45 minutes. Stir in cream and thyme. Puree in Blender or
with Immersion Blender until smooth. Add salt and pepper to taste.

sausage strata

This is another Christmas Tradition that we have every year with baked grits. This is best made the night before so that bread can absorb the liquid.

Ingredients

8 slices of bread, crusts removed

1 pound pork sausage, browned and crumbled

1 tablespoon prepared mustard

2 cups sharp cheddar cheese

2 cups milk

8 eggs

½ teaspoon salt

. . . .

*M*ix mustard with sausage. In 13x9x2 baking dish, layer bread, sausage and cheese. Blend together milk, eggs, salt and pepper.

Pour over sausage and bread.

Bake at 350° for 30 minutes or until knife inserted comes out clean.

This recipe freezes well!

breakfast casserole

My friend, Renee Harris, introduced this delicious dish to us. It has quickly become one of our favorites.

Ingredients

4 cups water

1 cup grits (uncooked)

1 pound bacon

7 eggs

1 package shredded cheddar cheese

½ cup (1 stick) butter

½ cup sour cream

. . . .

Cook grits in 4 cups of water. While grits are cooking, fry bacon and drain. Pour cooked grits in a casserole dish. Add sour cream and butter. Fry or scramble eggs. Chop up and place on top of grits. Crumble bacon and add to grits. Add ½ package of cheddar cheese. Mix well and spread out into dish. Top with remaining cheese. Bake at 350° for about 20 minutes until bubbly and cheese is melted.

*You may substitute ham or sausage for bacon.

quiche

When my sister Marilois got married, we went to a lovely party at our dear friend Anne Thomas' house. She served the most delicious quiches. I think she said she cut the recipes out of the newspaper. Even though the recipe is for crust less quiche, I prepared mine in a ready made pie crust.

Master Recipe

Ingredients

4 large eggs

½ cup evaporated milk

2 teaspoons Dijon mustard

½ teaspoon salt

¼ teaspoon ground black pepper

. . . .

Prepare filling ingredients and set aside. Grease a 9 inch Pyrex pie plate. Preheat oven to 400°. Whisk eggs, milk, mustard, salt and pepper. Stir in filling of choice (see following pages). Bake about 20 minutes until just set. Remove from oven and let rest 5 minutes.

bacon, leek & cheese quiche

Ingredients

½ pound sliced bacon, cut into 1 inch pieces

1 large leek, darkest green section trimmed, light green and white section quartered sliced thin and washed thoroughly

Scant ¼ teaspoon dried thyme leaves

6 oz Colby Jack or Swiss Cheese

• •

Heat a 12 inch skillet over medium-high heat. Add bacon and fry until crisp. Drain bacon in a small colander set over a bowl to catch the drippings. Return 2 tablespoons drippings to the skillet. Add leek. Saute until tender, 5 or 6 minutes, then scrape into colander with the bacon.

Add to Master recipe on page 67 and bake.

crab, corn & red pepper quiche

Ingredients

2 tablespoons olive oil

½ small red bell pepper, diced

2 cups frozen corn, thawed and drained

8 oz pasteurized lump crab meat, picked over

2 green onions, thinly sliced

5 oz (1 ¼ cups) grated Monterey Jack Cheese

1 oz (6 tablespoons) Parmesan Cheese

. . . .

Heat oil in 12-inch skillet over medium-high heat. Sauté pepper until just tender, 2 to 3 minutes, Add corn and sauté to heat through. Stir in crab and onions. Add to Master recipe on page 67 and bake.

spinach, mushrooms, tomatoes & feta quiche

3 tablespoons olive oil, divided

1 10 oz package sliced mushrooms

Salt and pepper, to taste

1 to 2 oz frozen chopped spinach, thawed and squeezed dry

12 cherry tomatoes, halved

2 green onions, thinly sliced

½ teaspoon dried oregano leaves

6 oz (1 ¼ cup) crumbled feta cheese.

. . . .

Heat 2 tablespoons oil in 12 inch skillet over medium high heat. Sauté mushrooms, seasoning with salt and pepper, until golden brown, about 5 minutes. Transfer to a bowl. Add remaining oil, spinach and tomatoes, seasoning with salt and pepper. Sauté to evaporate liquid, 2 to 3 minutes. Stir in onions. Add to mushrooms in bowl.

Add to Master Recipe on page 67 and Bake

sausage, cheddar, apple & sage quiche

Ingredients

8 oz sausage

1 large Granny Smith apple, peeled, cored and diced

½ teaspoon Dried rubbed sage

1 ½ cups sharp cheddar cheese, grated

. . . .

Brown sausage about 5 minutes, drain over bowl to catch drippings.

Return 2 tablespoons drippings to pan. Sauté apple until golden, about

3 –4 minutes. Add to colander.

Add to Master Recipe on page 67 and bake.

baked grits

My mom used to make these every Christmas when we were growing up. Her mother (my Mammy) made them before her. We make them at our house on Christmas morning now.

Ingredients

1 ¼ cup grits
1 ¼ teaspoon salt
3 ½ cups water
½ cup butter
6 (oz) Velveeta cheese
1 teaspoon garlic powder
1 cup milk
2 eggs
Tabasco Sauce
Grated cheddar cheese

. . . .

Boil grits and salt in water until done. Add butter, Velveeta and garlic powder. Add Tabasco sauce to taste. Stir in milk and eggs. Put into greased casserole dish and cook uncovered at 150 degrees for 45 minutes. Top with grated sharp cheddar cheese and bake 15 more minutes until brown.

fried grits

It seems that we often have grits left over when we cook them. My mom used to make these when we were children. My kids love them, too.

Ingredients

Leftover grits
1–2 eggs, slightly beaten

. . . .

*P*ack leftover grits in a drinking glass (preferably one that is the same diameter all the way down). Cover tightly and refrigerate overnight. Run a knife around the edge of the grits in the drinking glass to loosen. Dump out cylinder of grits and slice into ½ inch slices. Dip in beaten egg and brown in a skillet sprayed with cooking spray.

vegetables & side dishes

onion pie

Another favorite from my mom. This is great with a steak!

Ingredients

1 cup butter cracker crumbs

¼ cup butter, melted

2 cups thinly sliced onions

2 tablespoons butter

2 eggs

¾ cup milk

¾ teaspoon salt

dash of black pepper

¼ cup grated sharp Cheddar Cheese

. . . .

Mix cracker crumbs with ¼ cup melted butter. Press into 8-inch pie plate. Sauté onion in 2 tablespoons butter until translucent. Spoon into crust. Beat eggs with milk, salt and pepper. Pour over onions. Sprinkle with cheese. Bake, uncovered, at 350° for 30 minutes.

Garnish with parsley.

Yield: 6 to 8 servings

baked vidalia onion

Ingredients

1 large Vidalia onion per person

1 tablespoon butter (per onion)

½ teaspoon salt (per onion)

¼ teaspoon black pepper (per onion)

. . . .

Remove skin of onion and slice a small amount off of bottom of onion
to make it flat. Quarter onion almost cutting to the core.

Insert butter, salt and pepper.

Wrap onion individually in foil. Bake at 350 for an hour.

Serve in foil like a baked potato.

sweet potato souffle

Another award winning recipe from my friend Janet Wood. We have this every Thanksgiving!

Ingredients

3 cups cooked and mashed sweet potatoes

¾ cup sugar

2 eggs

1 tablespoon vanilla

½ cup melted butter

1 cup brown sugar

½ cup flour

1 cup chopped pecans

1/3 cup butter.

. . . .

Mix the first five ingredients and pour into 9 x 13 casserole dish. Mix next 4 ingredients with a fork and sprinkle on top of casserole.

Bake for 30 minutes at 350°.

twice baked potatoes

Ingredients

3–4 baking potatoes

¼ cup sour cream

¼ cup butter

½ cup cheddar cheese

2 tablespoons mayonnaise

2 tablespoons milk

. . . .

Bake potatoes until tender. Cut in half and hull out the potato.

Place empty hulls on a baking dish.

Mix potato, sour cream, butter, cheese, etc., to taste.

Spoon back into hull and bake at 450 for 15 minutes until browned.

baked potato topping

1 cup sharp cheddar cheese, grated

½ cup sour cream

¼ cup butter or margarine, softened

2 tablespoons chopped green onion.

. . . .

Combine all ingredients and serve on hot baked potatoes.

cheddar onion potatoes

Another classic from my Mom.

Ingredients

8 red skinned (or more) potatoes, washed but not peeled

1–2 thinly sliced onions

melted butter

cheddar cheese

salt and pepper

. . . .

Slice potatoes and layer with onion, butter cheese, salt and pepper.
Continue layering until baking dish is filled. (Fill it full because it will
shrink when it bakes). Top with cheddar cheese.
Bake, covered, at 350° until potatoes are tender.

mashed potatoes

Until I went to a Bible Study at friend Laura Murray's house, I had never seen anyone put Mayonnaise in mashed potatoes. Since then, I always add Mayonnaise to mine. It makes them smoother and adds great flavor.

Ingredients

3 pounds red potatoes, unpeeled
½ cup milk
3 tablespoons butter
½ cup sour cream
¼ cup mayonnaise
Salt and Pepper to taste

. . . .

Quarter potatoes and cook in salted water until tender. Drain and mash with potato masher. Add butter, milk, sour cream and mayo. Add more or less milk to desired consistency.

parmesan garlic mashed potatoes

3 pounds red potatoes, unpeeled

½ block cream cheese

2 tablespoons butter

2 tablespoons minced garlic

1 ½ cup grated Parmesan cheese

Salt and pepper

. . . .

Cook potatoes in salted water until tender. Drain and mash potatoes with potato masher. Add cream cheese, butter, garlic and Parmesan cheese, stirring until smooth.

dilly potato salad

Ingredients

3 pounds red potatoes, quartered

1 cup mayo

3 teaspoons dill

salt and pepper

2 tablespoons prepared mustard

3 dill pickles, minced

. . . .

Cook potatoes in salted water. Drain. Mix in mayo, mustard, dill, salt and pepper and pickles.

ranch squash casserole

This recipe is from our dear Aunt Rachael. It is a staple at ALL holiday gatherings!

Ingredients

2 lbs squash

1 cup onion, chopped

2 eggs

½ cup mayonnaise

½ cup sour cream

¾ cup milk

12 saltine crackers, crushed

1 (1 oz) pkg. powdered ranch dressing

1 cup grated cheddar cheese

1–2 cups buttered bread crumbs

. . . .

Boil squash and onion until tender. Drain. Mix all other ingredients except bread crumbs. Fold into squash and onions. Mix well and pour into 9 x 13 casserole dish. Top with bread crumbs. Bake at 350° for 45–55 minutes, until hot and brown.

squash casserole

This recipe is from my mother-in-law, Elizabeth.

Ingredients

4 cups cooked squash, drained and chopped

1 cup mayo

3 eggs

1 medium onion, chopped

1 can cream of chicken or mushroom soup

1 cup grated cheese

cracker crumbs for topping

. . . .

*M*ix all ingredients except crumbs. Pour into greased casserole dish.

Top with crumbs and bake at 350 for 25–30 minutes.

broccoli casserole

Ingredients

1 bag chopped broccoli
1 can cream of mushroom or cream of chicken soup
1 8 oz. tub of sour cream
grated cheddar cheese

. . . .

Cook broccoli and drain. Mix soup and sour cream. Stir in broccoli
and pour into casserole dish. Top with grated cheese.

Bake at 350° for 25–30 minutes.

*You may use broccoli and cauliflower for a different taste.

lemon green beans

Ingredients

1 package green beans
1 tablespoon butter or margarine
seasoning salt
dash of lemon juice

. . . .

Cook beans according to package until tender. Drain and return to
pot. Add butter, seasoning salt (to taste) and lemon juice.

roasted asparagus

Ingredients

1 package fresh asparagus
cooking spray
garlic salt or seasoning salt

. . . .

Spray baking sheet with cooking spray. Arrange asparagus in single
layer. Spray asparagus with cooking spray and sprinkle with salt.
Bake at 450° 10 minutes.

honeyed carrots

1 package frozen carrots
2 tablespoons butter
4 tablespoons honey
½ teaspoon salt

. . . .

Cook carrots until tender in salted water. Drain. Mix in butter, honey and salt. Place back in pot on stove for a few minutes (stirring constantly) until glazed in appearance.

fried rice

Ingredients

2 cups cooked white rice

2 eggs

soy sauce

green onions, chopped

oil

. . . .

"Fry" eggs in a little oil in a large skillet or wok and chop up. Add rice
and brown slightly. Add onions and soy sauce. Serve Hot.
Add cooked shrimp, chicken, beef or pork to make a main dish.

brown rice

This is a favorite from my friend Liane Register.

Ingredients

¾ stick butter

1 medium onion, chopped

1 cup rice uncooked

2 cans beef broth

. . . .

Brown rice in skillet in butter.

Transfer to baking dish and stir in chopped onion and soup.

Microwave 25 minutes stirring every 10 minutes.

brown rice II

This is another brown rice recipe that is great, too.

Ingredients

1 cup uncooked rice

½ stick butter

1 can beef broth

1 can French Onion Soup

1 jar sliced mushrooms

. . . .

Brown rice in butter. Pour into covered baking dish and add soups and
mushrooms. Bake at 350° for 1 hour.

cornbread dressing

I ran across this recipe several years ago on the internet. It has been a Thanksgiving staple ever since. SO so good!

Ingredients

4 cups of cornbread, crumbled (I use Jiffy cornbread mix)

3 or 4 biscuits crumbled

2 cans (13 ¾ oz) chicken broth

1 large onion, chopped

1 ½ ribs celery, chopped

3 eggs

1 cup melted butter

. . . .

Combine biscuits, cornbread and broth. Allow to soak. Add onion, celery and egg and mix. Add melted butter. Pour into 9 x 13 dish.
Bake at 350° for 1 hour and 20 minutes.

orange congealed salad

Someone brought this congealed salad to us when my Mammy passed away in 1994. We've been making it ever since. It is a holiday staple also.

Ingredients

1 package lemon gelatin
1 package orange gelatin
2 cups boiling water
2 cans drained mandarin oranges
1 large can crushed pineapple (undrained)
miniature marshmallows
1 cup Mayonnaise
1 small tub cool whip
cheddar cheese

. . . .

Mix water, gelatin and fruit in 9 X 13 casserole dish. While hot, top
with mini marshmallows. Refrigerate until firm.
Mix mayo and cool whip. Spread over gelatin and marshmallows.
Sprinkle with cheddar cheese.

sour cherry salad

This recipe is from family friend Anne Thomas.

Ingredients

1 package lemon gelatin
1 tablespoon plain gelatin
1 can tart pie cherries
1 small can crushed pineapple
1 cup sugar
juice and zest of 1 lemon
juice of 1 orange
1 cup pecans OR walnuts

. . . .

Drain cherries and pineapple. Save juice. Heat (but do not boil)
cherry and pineapple juice. Dissolve plain and lemon gelatin. Add
sugar, lemon and orange juice. Chill until syrupy consistency.
Add other ingredients and chill.

grape salad

This recipe is from my friend Alison Smith.

Ingredients

4 lbs red and/or green grapes

1 block cream cheese

1 8 oz sour cream

1 cup sugar

1 teaspoon vanilla extract

Topping:

1 cup chopped pecans

¾ cup brown sugar

. . . .

Mix and pour into casserole dish.

Combine pecans and brown sugar. Sprinkle over grapes. Chill.

ambrosia

One of the things I remember most about my Mammy was her Ambrosia. She loved to make it for family gatherings.

Ingredients

1 peeled apple
2 bananas
1 small can orange juice
1 orange juice can of water
1 (20 oz) can pineapple chunks
1 package coconut

. . . .

*M*ix all of the above and serve chilled.

pineapple casserole

Our annual Easter Egg hunt yields a bevy of wonderful dishes such as this casserole from Prissy McLaine.

Ingredients

20 **ounces crushed pineapple**

½ **cup sugar**

3 **tablespoons flour**

1 **cup grated cheddar cheese**

¼ **cup melted butter**

1 **sleeve crushed butter crackers**

. . . .

Mix pineapple, sugar, flour and cheese. Spoon into 1 quart casserole dish. Combine cracker crumbs and butter. Sprinkle over pineapple. Bake at 350 for 25 minutes.

salad

Ingredients

1 pound (1 head) iceberg lettuce

1 pound spinach or Bibb lettuce

1 pound bacon, cooked and crumbled

fresh mushrooms (½ of 8oz box)

3–4 hard boiled eggs

Dressing

½ cup Mazola oil

¼ cup cider vinegar

2 tablespoons sugar

1 tablespoon poppy seed

2 tablespoons minced onion

1 teaspoon brown Dijon mustard

¾ cup large curd cottage cheese

. . . .

Shake all ingredients and pour over salad
(do not add cottage cheese until serving time).

southwestern layered salad

This is a low fat recipe. It is SO good and beautiful in a glass bowl.

Ingredients

1 can black beans, drained and rinsed

¼ cup salsa

2 cups finely chopped romaine lettuce

2 medium tomatoes, chopped

1 can whole kernel corn, drained

1 green bell pepper, seeded and diced

1 red onion, finely chopped

½ cup reduced fat cheddar cheese

½ avocado, peeled and cut into ¼ inch slices

2 slices reduced sodium bacon, cooked and crumbled

¼ cup fat free Italian dressing

. . . .

Layer above items in a 1 ½ quart clear bowl in above order. Just before serving, arrange avocado on top, sprinkle with bacon and drizzle with dressing.

oriental chicken salad/ slaw

This recipe comes from my cousin Karen Parrott in Spartanburg, SC. We love this during the summer!

Ingredients

4 boneless skinless chicken breasts

1 package Romaine Hearts Lettuce

2 packages Oriental Ramen Noodles (uncooked)

¼ cup toasted almond slivers

spring onions

. . . .

Cook chicken in skillet until no longer pink. Cut or shred into small pieces. Wash and cut (or shred) lettuce into large salad bowl. Pour chicken over greens. Crush uncooked noodles and sprinkle over chicken; add chopped onion and almonds.

Top with oriental dressing immediately before serving.

oriental dressing

Ingredients

½ Cup oil

¼ cup vinegar

1 tablespoon sugar

1 package of seasoning from Ramen Noodles.

. . . .

Mix well and pour over salad.

strawberry walnut salad

My friend Amanda James introduced us to this delicious salad.

Ingredients

1 package Romaine Hearts, washed and torn into small pieces
1 package shredded Monterey Jack Cheese
2 pints Strawberries, sliced
1 cup Walnuts

. . . .

Layer romaine, cheese, berries and walnuts.
Top with vinaigrette dressing just before serving.

vinaigrette dressing

Ingredients

¾ cup sugar

½ cup Red Wine Vinegar

1 cup Oil

¼ teaspoon White Pepper

2 cloves minced garlic

½ teaspoon paprika

½ teaspoon salt

. . . .

*M*ix in large jar and chill before serving.

tomato pie

My mom used to make this when we were younger. It is great!

Ingredients

1 deep dish pie crust

4 fresh tomatoes

4 pieces crumbled bacon

1 cup shredded cheddar cheese

½ scant cup mayonnaise

. . . .

Bake crust until soft brown. Slice tomatoes into pan and top with
Bacon. Mix cheese and mayonnaise. Spread over bacon and tomatoes.
Bake until cheese is melted and browned.

tomato basil pie

This recipe comes from my cousin Karen Parrott.

Ingredients

1 **frozen pie crust**

2 **ripe tomatoes**

2–3 **leaves fresh basil**

1 **teaspoon olive oil**

¼ **cup mozzarella cheese**

. . . .

Remove pie crust from pie plate and place on baking sheet. Slice
tomatoes over crust. Top with chopped fresh basil and cheese.
Drizzle with olive oil. Bake at 350° for 20 minutes or until browned.

beef, poultry, pork & seafood

soppy shrimp

My mom gave me this recipe. She got it from family friend Frances Hatcher. Named Soppy Shrimp, because you use the French Bread to "sop" up all of the juice. You peel these as you eat them after they have absorbed all of the delicious flavor.

Ingredients

6 lbs fresh shrimp, in shells
1 large bottle Italian dressing
1 ½ lemons juiced
Worcestershire sauce
2–3 shakes Tabasco sauce
1 cup minced garlic
4 sticks butter
2 loaves of French bread

. . . .

Mix ingredients (except for shrimp and bread) and bring to a boil. Simmer for 20 minutes. Wash shrimp in shell and place in large casserole dish. Pour sauce over shrimp and top with lemon slices. Bake for 40 minutes.

shrimp boil or low country boil

Ingredients

Old bay seasoning (about ¼ cup)

several pounds of shrimp (in shell), washed

large pork sausage cut into 3 inch (or so) pieces

red potatoes, washed

small corn on the cob

. . . .

In large boiling pot, boil water and lots of old bay seasoning.
Add potatoes and cook until tender. Add sausage and corn and cook
for about 8–10 minutes. Add shrimp and boil for another 3–5 minutes
or until shrimp are pink. You may adjust the amount of Old Bay
depending on how spicy you want it.

crab casserole

This is one of my grandmother's prized recipes. I can understand why.

Ingredients

2 pounds crab meat

8 tablespoons butter

7 tablespoons flour

2 cups evaporated milk

2 tablespoons prepared mustard

4 tablespoons lemon juice

4 boiled eggs

1 cup mayonnaise

1 onion, grated

dash Tabasco sauce

Cracker crumbs

butter

. . . .

Melt butter in saucepan and gradually whisk in flour blending until smooth. Slowly add evaporated milk to make a thick cream sauce. Remove from heat and add crab meat, mustard, lemon juice, eggs, mayonnaise, onion and Tabasco to taste. Pour into greased 9 x 13 casserole dish. Top with crushed cracker crumbs and dot with butter. Bake at 350° for 30 minutes until hot and bubbly.

shrimp and rice

I can remember many family gatherings that my grandmother made this dish.

Ingredients

1 ½ pounds shrimp

1 can cream of mushroom soup

¾ cup sharp cheddar cheese

1 cup vinegar

5 cups water

2 teaspoons garlic salt

2–3 tablespoons cooking sherry

. . . .

Boil shrimp in vinegar and water until pink. Drain and sprinkle with Garlic salt. Warm soup and melt cheese in it. Add shrimp and sherry. Serve over rice.

the best meat marinade

Ingredients

2 teaspoon Minced garlic

1 tablespoon brown sugar

½ teaspoon pepper

1 tablespoon oil

1 tablespoon water

1 cup **soy sauce**

. . . .

*M*ix together and marinate any meat for several hours or overnight for best results. Cook on grill.

*¼ teaspoon ginger can be added for a more Asian flavor.

teriyaki grilled salmon

This recipe is from my friend, Jenny Robbins. I gave my friend Caroline Lankford the recipe and she made it for Jenny and her family one night. Jenny raved and raved about how delicious and asked Caroline for the recipe.

Ingredients

4 **salmon steaks**

¼ **cup brown sugar**

3 **tablespoons olive oil**

3 **tablespoons soy sauce**

1 **and ½ tablespoons minced garlic**

1 **and ½ tablespoons minced fresh ginger**

. . . .

Marinate steaks in a zippered freezer bag for several hours or overnight. Grill for 6–8 minutes per inch of thickness of steak.

bami's chicken pie

This recipe comes from my great Aunt Bami. It is one of our favorites to take to friends.

Ingredients

One whole chicken, cooked and de-boned
1 can chicken broth
1 can cream of chicken soup
3 hard boiled eggs

Crust:
1 cup self rising flour
¾ cup milk
1 stick melted butter

. . . .

Cook and de-bone chicken. Place chicken cut into bite-sized pieces in a 9 x 13 casserole dish. Mix chicken broth and cream of chicken soup and pour over chicken in pan. Slice eggs and place over chicken mixture. Mix crust and spoon over chicken. Do not stir.

Bake at 350° for 1 hour.

swiss chicken

4–6 boneless-skinless chicken breasts

8 slices Swiss cheese

1 can cream of mushroom soup

½ soup can of white wine

¾ cup stuffing mix

¼ cup butter (melted)

. . . .

Place chicken breasts in a greased baking dish, top with slices of Swiss cheese. Mix soup and wine. Pour over chicken. Sprinkle stuffing mix over top and drizzle with butter. Bake at 350° for 45–55 minutes

lemon basil chicken

Ingredients

1 package boneless, skinless chicken breasts
salt and pepper
4 teaspoons lemon juice
8 lemon slices
2 tablespoons fresh basil

. . . .

Place each chicken breast on a piece of aluminum foil. Top with salt and pepper, 1 teaspoon of lemon juice, 2 lemon slices and a tablespoon of fresh basil. Wrap in foil and cook on a grill until done (about 20 minutes). This could be done in the oven, also. Cooking on about 450 for 20 minutes or until done.

easy chicken enchiladas

Ingredients

8–6 inch flour tortillas

melted butter

2 cups diced cooked chicken (cooked with chili powder in the water)

¾ cup sliced black olives

1 cup Monterey Jack or Cheddar cheese

Sauce:

1 clove garlic

1 tablespoon olive oil

2 cans tomato sauce

1 cup water

1 ½ teaspoons chili powder

. . . .

Brush tortillas with butter on both sides. Pile ¼ cup chicken, a tablespoon of olives and a sprinkling of cheese. Roll up and place side by side in a greased casserole dish. Sauté garlic in oil. Add tomato sauce, water and chili powder. Pour over rolls and top with additional olives and cheese. Bake at 350° for 15–20 minutes. Serves 4

pecan chicken

Ingredients

1 package (4–6) boneless, skinless chicken breasts
½ cup toasted bread crumbs
½ cup pecans
milk
butter
garlic salt
pepper

. . . .

Blend pecans in food processor until fine. Mix with bread crumbs and pour into shallow dish with garlic salt and dash of pepper. Dredge chicken breasts in milk and then in bread crumb/pecan mixture. Brown in skillet in butter and cook over medium heat until thoroughly cooked (approx 7 minutes on each side).

chicken crescent puffs

This recipe was originally given to me by family friend Kristy Tillman Hunt. I changed it a little to make individual puffs.

Ingredients

1 pkg. boneless skinless chicken breasts, cooked and shredded

2 (8oz) package cream cheese

½ teaspoons salt

1/8 teaspoons pepper

3 tablespoons milk

¼ cup chopped onion

3 can crescent rolls

. . . .

Preheat oven to 350. Mix chicken, cream cheese, salt, pepper, milk and onions. Spoon small amount of chicken mixture onto wide end of each triangle of crescent rolls. Roll triangles around chicken mixture and seal edges. Place point down in muffin tins.
Bake 20 to 25 minutes until brown. Makes 24 puffs.

poppy seed chicken

I think this is the only recipe I've ever gotten from my domestically challenged sister Marilois. You'd never know she didn't like to cook much based on this delicious recipe.

Ingredients

1 pound cooked chicken breasts
8 oz sour cream
1 can cream of chicken soup
1 sleeve butter crackers, crushed
poppy seeds

. . . .

Shred chicken and cover bottom of casserole dish. Mix sour cream
and soup. Spread over chicken and sprinkle cracker crumbs over top.
Sprinkle with poppy seeds.
Bake at 375 for 30–45 minutes until brown and bubbly.

wine chicken

Ingredients

4 boneless, skinless chicken breasts

1 can cream of mushroom soup

¾ (soup can) of white wine

butter

. . . .

Brown chicken breasts in butter (seasoning with salt and pepper).
Place chicken in 9 x 13 pan and pour drippings over chicken. Mix
soup and wine and pour over chicken. Cover and bake at 350° for 1
hour. Serve with rice and use soup for gravy. Delicious!

This is also great in the crock pot.

Cook on low for 8–10 hours or on high 4–5 hours.

chicken and dumplings

There is no better southern comfort food than Chicken and Dumplings. This is an easy recipe because there are now frozen dumplings that are every bit as good as homemade.

Ingredients

1 whole chicken
2 carrots, sliced
2 stalks celery, sliced
1 small onion, diced
1 package frozen dumplings
salt and pepper

. . . .

Put chicken in large boiling pot and cover with water. Salt and pepper water well. Add carrots, celery and onion. Boil chicken for about 45 minutes until chicken is cooked. De-bone chicken and remove vegetables from stock. Return chicken meat to stock and bring to a boil. Add frozen dumplings and cook, covered, about 20 minutes. If you want to make this after work and do not have time to boil the chicken, the chicken can be cooked in a crock pot (4–5 hours on high or 6–8 hours on low) and will be ready when you get home.

chicken and rice

Chicken and Rice is another great southern comfort food.

Ingredients

1 whole chicken
2 carrots, diced
2 stalks, celery, diced
1 small onion, diced
1 ½ cups rice
salt and pepper

. . . .

Put chicken in large boiling pot and cover with water. Salt and pepper water well. Add vegetables. Boil chicken for about 45 minutes until chicken is cooked. De-bone chicken and remove vegetables from stock. Return chicken meat to 3 ½ cups of stock and bring to a boil. Add rice and cook, covered, about 20 minutes. If you want to make this after work and do not have time to boil the chicken, the chicken can be cooked in a crock pot (4–5 hours on high or 6–8 hours on low) and will be ready when you get home.

honey mustard chicken salad

Ingredients

4–6 boneless skinless chicken breasts

spring onions (chopped)

1 large snack box of raisins

¼ cup chopped pecans

Honey Mustard dipping sauce (recipe follows)

salt

pepper

. . . .

Boil chicken breasts until no longer pink (10–15 minutes); cut into small pieces or shred. Mix with onions, raisins, pecans and honey mustard sauce. Salt and pepper to taste.

Excellent on lettuce or on a croissant.

honey mustard dipping sauce

Ingredients

½ cup mayonnaise

3 tablespoons prepared mustard

3 tablespoons honey

. . . .

Stir all ingredients together until fully mixed.
This is great for dipping chicken tenders, too.

chicken florentine

1 package boneless, skinless chicken breasts

1 (8 oz) tub sour cream

1 package frozen spinach

1 can cream of mushroom soup

½ soup can of white wine

1 cup mayonnaise

1 ½ cup Cheddar cheese

dash lemon juice

salt and pepper

· ·

Boil chicken until done. Cut into bite sized pieces. Cook spinach and drain. Mix chopped chicken and spinach in 9 x 13 casserole dish. Mix wine, soup, sour cream, mayo, ¾ cup of cheese, lemon juice, salt and pepper and pour over spinach and chicken. Mix well. Top with remaining cheese and bake at 350° for 30 minutes until bubbly.

mammy's beef and chicken

We were first introduced to this dish at friend Gail Blitch's house. Recently my Aunt Pat Wainer gave me my Mammy's recipe cards. My Mammy must have really liked this recipe because it was in there three separate times. It IS delicious!

Ingredients

8 boned chicken breasts
1 package dried beef
8 strips of bacon (partially cooked)
1 can cream of mushroom soup
½ pint sour cream

. . . .

Layer beef in bottom of casserole dish. Wrap bacon around chicken and place on top of beef. Mix soup and sour cream. Pour over chicken.

Bake, uncovered, at 225° for 3 hours.

ham and potato casserole

Another great one from friend Liane Register.

Ingredients

32 oz package square hash browns

½ cup chopped onion

8 oz sour cream

1 can cream of potato soup

½ soup can of milk

1 package grated cheese (for in the casserole and on top)

½ teaspoon pepper

1 teaspoon salt

1 pound diced ham

. . . .

Mix all of the above ingredients and put into a 9 x 13 baking dish.

Bake at 350° for 1 hour.

baked ham

Ingredients

1 (8–10 pound) smoked ham

½ cup brown sugar

2 tablespoons prepared mustard

. . . .

Place ham in baking dish and cover with foil. Bake at 325° for 20 minutes per pound. With about 30 minutes left on cooking time, mix sugar and mustard. Spread over ham. Return to oven and bake, uncovered, remaining 30 minutes or until internal temperature reaches 140°.

pork tenderloin

Ingredients

1 (1 pound) pork tenderloin
"The Best Meat Marinade" (p. 114)

. . . .

Marinate 6 hours (or overnight) in The Best Meat Marinade (page 114). Grill 20 minutes per pound or until no longer pink and internal temperature reaches 140–145 degrees.

stampot

My sister Katharine is living in the Netherlands. This is a traditional dish from the Netherlands that my mom says is delicious! Stampot is one traditional dish from the Netherlands. It is a hearty meal made with simple, basic ingredients that can be enjoyed throughout the winter. During World War II, the Dutch reduced the amount of potatoes and mixed in rice to stretch the portions. This recipe excerpt is from the *Kook and Huishoud Boek,* the *Cook and Domestic Book* by Wilma Munch, teacher from the Agricultural Domestic Training Program, published in 1950. It was modernized with help from Katharine's next door neighbor.

Ingredients

6 **large carrots**
2–2 ½ lbs. **Peeled potatoes**
3 **large onions**
bouillon
salt and pepper
Smoked Sausage

. . . .

Cut onions into large dice; peel and slice the carrots and potatoes into even-sized pieces. Cook everything together in broth for an hour or until soft and mashable. There should be enough liquid that when the vegetables are cooked, the whole pot can be mashed together. Season with salt and pepper and serve with smoked or regular sausage. As an option, you may mash with the potatoes (instead of carrots) things such as sauerkraut, savoy cabbage, apples, pears or endive.

Eet smakelijk!

pizza casserole

Ingredients

1 Package ground beef
1 jar spaghetti sauce
1 small package mozzarella cheese
1 can canned Biscuits

. . . .

Brown ground beef and drain. Pour into casserole dish and stir in spaghetti sauce. Sprinkle cheese over beef mixture. Separate (peel apart) biscuits into thirds and place over the top of the cheese. Bake according to directions on biscuit can until brown.

low fat meatloaf

Ingredients

½ cup ketchup

½ cup oatmeal

¼ cup minced onion (or you can use a packet of onion soup mix)

2 eggs

2 pounds lean ground beef

dash of Worcestershire sauce

salt and pepper (omit salt if you use onion soup mix)

. . . .

Preheat oven to 350°. Combine ingredients in a large bowl. Shape into a loaf shape in a loaf pan. Top with additional ketchup.

Bake at 350° for an hour and ten minutes. You may also make these in individual muffin tins, cooking them for about 20 minutes or until done. The extras may be frozen for a quick meal.

mom's best spaghetti

Ingredients

2 –3 strips of bacon

1–2 tablespoons olive oil

2 small onions, chopped

1 clove garlic

2–3 pounds ground beef

large jar spaghetti sauce

. . . .

Brown bacon in large cooking pot. Add oil and onions and cook until onions are translucent. Stir in garlic and ground beef. Cook beef until browned. Add sauce. Simmer for around an hour, stirring occasionally. Salt to taste. Serve over Angel Hair Pasta.

wetbacks
(taco salad in a bag)

Ingredients

4 snack sized bags of taco chips

1 small package of ground beef

lettuce

grated cheddar cheese

sour cream

tomatoes

black olives

salsa

. . . .

*B*rown ground beef and drain. Slit bags of chips lengthwise and peel
back (leaving bags flat and chips inside.
Top chips with ground beef and other desired items.

beef tips

Ingredients

1 package beef tips
1 can beef broth
1 soup can of red wine
1 envelope onion soup mix.

• • • • • • • • • • • • • • • • • • •

*P*ut beef in crock pot and add other ingredients. Stir well. Cook on low heat 8–10 hours or high heat 4–5 hours. Serve over rice or mashed potatoes. This is tender, delicious and my family loves it!

flank steak marinade

This recipe is from Jenny Robbins' sister Angel Hobby. She describes it as so tender, you don't have to have teeth to eat it

Ingredients

1 flank steak

¾ cup olive oil

½ cup soy sauce

2 tablespoons vinegar

2 tablespoons honey

1 ½ tablespoons fresh ginger

1 teaspoon garlic

1 scallion

. . . .

Mix all ingredients.

Marinate at least overnight and grill over hot coals turning once.

cookies, bars & candies

the best brownies you'll ever eat

I came up with this recipe in college. It is STILL one of our favorites, especially Laci's.

Ingredients

1 box fudge brownies

3 Toffee candy bars, crushed (or you can use Heath Bites candy) delete

1 teaspoon instant coffee powder

1 tablespoon hot water

1 (4 oz) package cream cheese, softened

1 jar marshmallow creme

. . . .

Bake brownies according to directions on box being careful not to over bake. Immediately upon removal from oven, sprinkle crushed toffee bars over hot brownies. Cool. Dissolve coffee powder in hot water. Blend in cream cheese. Fold in marshmallow creme. Spread over cooled brownies. Chill.

not yo' mama's brownies

Ingredients

2 packages brownie mix

3 LARGE Symphony bars with toffee and almonds

. . . .

*M*ix one box of brownies and pour into greased 9 x 13 pan. Top with
layer of symphony bars (3 should fit perfectly into pan). Mix other box
of brownies and pour over symphony bars. Bake according to 8 inch
pan directions on brownie box (longest baking time).

chocolate mint brownies

Ingredients

1 package brownie mix

1 ½ cups powdered sugar

3 tablespoons butter, softened

2 tablespoons whipping cream

¾ teaspoons peppermint extract

2 drops green food coloring

2 (1 oz) squares baking chocolate

2 tablespoons butter

1 teaspoon vanilla

. . . .

Bake brownies according to box directions. Cool. Mix powdered sugar, butter, whipping cream, extract and food coloring. Spread over cooled brownies and chill for 1 hour. Melt baking chocolate and butter in microwave. Stir in vanilla. Drizzle over peppermint layer. Chill 1 hour.

blondies

Ingredients

½ cup margarine softened

1 (16 oz) package light brown sugar

3 eggs

2 cups self rising flour

1 teaspoon vanilla

1 cup chopped nuts

. . . .

Cream together margarine and sugar. Add eggs and beat well. Add
flour, vanilla and nuts. Pour into 13x9x2 greased baking dish and bake
at 300° for 45 minutes. This recipe is great topped with a scoop of
vanilla ice cream, caramel sauce and chopped pecans.

cream cheese bars

Ingredients

1 Box yellow cake mix

1 stick butter, softened

1 egg

1 (8 oz) cream cheese

2 eggs

1 box powdered sugar

. . . .

Mix cake mix, butter and 1 egg. Press into 9 x 13 casserole dish.
Blend cream cheese, 2 remaining eggs and powdered sugar with electric mixer until well blended. Pour over crust.

Bake at 350° for 30 minutes.

7 layer bars

Ingredients

¼ cup plus 1 tablespoon butter

1 ½ cups graham cracker crumbs (I use cinnamon ones)

1 cup flaked coconut

1 cup semi-sweet chocolate chips (or chunks)

1 cup butterscotch morsels (optional)

1 cup chopped pecans

1 (15 oz) can sweetened condensed milk.

. . . .

Place butter in 9 inch square baking pan and bake at 325° degrees until melted. Remove from oven. Layer cracker crumbs, coconut, chocolate chips, butterscotch and pecans with melted butter (do not stir) Spread condensed milk over top. Bake at 325° for 30 minutes. Cut into 1 ½ inch squares and remove to wire racks to cool.

peanut butter oat bars

Jody's step-mom, Debby, brought these on a beach picnic this summer. I was asking for the recipe before we got home! They are SO delicious.

Ingredients

2/3 cup butter
¼ cup peanut butter
1 cup packed brown sugar
¼ cup light corn syrup
¼ teaspoon vanilla
4 cups quick cooking oats

. . . .

Combine above ingredients and press into greased 9 x 13 baking dish.
Bake at 400° for 12–14 minutes. Cool 5 minutes.
Melt in the microwave or in a saucepan the following:

1 cup milk chocolate chips
½ cup butterscotch chips
1/3 cup peanut butter
Spread over bars and cool completely.

brown sugar cookies

Another recipe of my Bami's passed down through my mom.

Ingredients

1 **cup real butter**

1 **cup light brown sugar, packed**

4 **cups all purpose flour**

1 **cup chopped pecans**

2 **teaspoons vanilla**

100 **pecan halves**

. . . .

Cream butter and sugar; add nuts and vanilla: slowly beat in flour. Pat into 4 square (8 x 8) or 2 long (9 x 13) pans. Use a knife to score your batter into squares (5 rows and columns) before baking. Press a pecan half into each square. Bake in pre-heated 350° oven for 30 minutes. Sprinkle with granulated sugar as soon as you remove from oven. Cut into squares while hot, let cool in pan.

peanut butter reeses cup cookies

My mom used to make these for us as an after school snack. It is still a favorite of ours!

Ingredients

1 roll chocolate chip or peanut butter cookie dough
48 mini chocolate peanut butter cups

. . . .

Slice cookie dough into 1 inch slices and cut into fourths. Place dough into greased mini-muffin tins. Bake according to directions on dough roll. While the cookies are baking, unwrap peanut butter cups. Press one peanut butter cup into each cookie as soon as it comes out of the oven. Cool in pans.

oatmeal cookies

This recipe is another of my Grandmother's. There is not a better oatmeal cookie recipe out there.

Ingredients

1 cup butter flavored Crisco
1 cup brown sugar
1 cup white sugar
2 eggs, beaten
1 teaspoon vanilla
1 teaspoon almond extract
1 ½ cup self rising flour
1 teaspoon salt
1 teaspoon soda
1 teaspoon cinnamon
1 teaspoon ginger
3 cups oatmeal
1 cup raisins (optional)

. . . .

Cream shortening and sugar. Add eggs. Sift flour and dry ingredients. Add to other mixture. Add flavorings. Beat until smooth. Stir in oatmeal and raisins. Drop by teaspoons onto cookie sheet.

Bake at 350° 8–10 minutes.

reindeer cookies

Ingredients

1 package peanut butter cookie dough
pretzels
chocolate chips
red hot candies

. . . .

Cut cookie dough into slices and place 2 inches apart on a cookie sheet. Indent circle to make it look like a face. Place pretzels at the top of the cookie to resemble antlers. Place chocolate chips to resemble eyes and a red hot to resemble a nose. Bake according to directions on cookie dough.

two tone butter cookies

These cookies are delicious and are great because they are frozen and can quickly be baked for unexpected holiday company.

Ingredients

1 cup butter
1 cup confectioners sugar
1 teaspoon vanilla extract
2 cups all purpose flour
red and green food coloring

. . . .

In mixing bowl, cream butter and sugar. Beat in vanilla. Add flour and mix well. Divide dough in half. Tint half red and half green with food coloring. Roll dough portions to 1/8 inch, equal sized oblong shapes. Place one color on top of the other and roll starting with the long side (jelly roll style) into a long cylinder.
Wrap in plastic wrap and freeze for up to six months.

To prepare cookies: Let dough stand at room temperature for 15 minutes. Cut into slices. Bake on ungreased cookie sheet at 350 for 12–14 minutes.

candy cane cookies

My mom found this recipe in a magazine when we were children.
We have made them every Christmas since.

Ingredients

½ cup shortening

½ cup butter

1 cup powdered sugar

1 egg, beaten

1 teaspoon almond extract

1 teaspoon peppermint extract

2 ½ cups all purpose flour

1 teaspoon salt

½ tablespoon red food coloring

½ cup crushed peppermint

½ cup sugar

. . . .

Mix shortening, butter, sugar, egg and extracts. Mix in flour and salt.
Divide and tint half red. Roll and twist into 4" rope and bend one end
to form a candy cane shape. Bake on ungreased cookie 375° for 9 minutes. Upon removing from oven, sprinkle with
peppermint and sugar.

shortbread cookies

This recipe is from our family friend Janet Strickland. Every February I get a hankering to make these cookies. She serves them sometimes as a dessert sandwiched with home-made whipped cream and topped with raspberry puree.

Ingredients

1 pound butter

1 cup sugar

5 cups all purpose flour

. . . .

Cream butter and sugar. Gradually add flour. Roll to ¼ inch
thickness on waxed paper. Cut into desired shapes.
Bake on ungreased cookie sheet at 300° for 30 minutes.

marmalade drop cookies

Ingredients

½ cup butter

1 cup sugar

1 egg

3 cups self rising flour

1 cup orange marmalade.

. . . .

Cream butter and sugar until fluffy. Stir in beaten egg. Add flour then marmalade. Mix thoroughly. Drop by teaspoon on greased baking sheet. Bake at 350° 8–10 minutes until brown.

butter spritz cookies

Ingredients

½ cup butter

½ cup shortening

¾ cup sugar

I egg

2 ¼ cups all purpose flour

½ teaspoon baking powder

½ teaspoon salt

I teaspoon almond extract

. . . .

Cream butter, shortening and sugar. Add egg and almond extract.

Combine flour, baking powder and salt and add to butter mixture.

Press onto ungreased baking sheets using a cookie press.

Bake at 400° for 10–12 minutes until browned.

cream cheese spritz cookies

1 cup butter

1 (8 oz) package cream cheese

2/3 cup sugar

1 teaspoon vanilla

2 cups all purpose flour

dash of salt

. . . .

Cream butter, cream cheese and sugar. Add vanilla, salt and flour.

Press onto ungreased cookie sheet using a cookie press.

Bake at 400° 8 –10 minutes until browned.

peppermint bark

I make this for friends and family every Christmas. I always get calls the next year for the recipe.

Ingredients

1 package white chocolate chips
4 candy canes

. . . .

Melt white chocolate in the microwave. Stir after 40 seconds and microwave in 30 second increments stirring after each time. Put candy canes in a ziploc bag and crush with a rolling pin or beat with a measuring cup. Stir peppermint into melted chocolate and spread on waxed paper. Once bark hardens, break into small pieces to serve.

party mints

Ingredients

1 block cream cheese

1 stick butter

2 pounds confectioners sugar

1 teaspoon peppermint extract

few drops of red food coloring

. . . .

Mix all ingredients until stiff (use more sugar if needed). Using cookie
press with decorating tip or decorators bag, squeeze into desired size
on waxed paper. Allow to dry. Store in airtight container.

Makes 200 mints

chocolate covered cherries

We love to prepare homemade treats for the Holidays. These cherries are delicious and so easy the kids can help make them.

Ingredients

4 cups confectioners sugar

1 can Eagle Brand Milk

1 stick butter

1 teaspoon vanilla

1 large jar cherries with stems (drained and dried)

1 package Bakers Chocolate

1 sheet paraffin wax

. . . .

Melt butter, add milk and vanilla. Blend in sugar. Pinch off and flatten. Work around Cherries. Melt chocolate and paraffin in microwave. Dip cherries in chocolate and place on waxed paper to dry.

caramels

Ingredients

4 cups sugar

3 cups corn syrup

2 cups water

2 cups evaporated milk

1 tablespoon vanilla

. . . .

*P*ut sugar, syrup and one half of the milk and one half of the water in a large pot and boil, stirring constantly, until candy thermometer reaches 236° or test in cold water for soft ball stage. When it reaches this stage, pour in the remaining milk and water and cook to 242° (firm ball stage). Turn onto well oiled slab or platter. Cool and cut into 1 inch squares. Caramels must be wrapped individually.

pralines

This is a recipe of my Aunt Bami's.

Ingredients

2 cups light brown sugar

¼ cup hot water

pinch salt

large lump of butter (to butter pan)

1 teaspoon vanilla

1 cup pecan

. . . .

Boil sugar, water, and salt in large saucepan for 5 minutes. Add vanilla. Beat 1 minute. Stir in pecans. Drop on buttered paper or platter.

easter story cookies

We LOVE to make these at Easter. These delicious cookies also double as dessert for our Easter dinner. They are great served as a side with Sherbet or other homemade ice cream.

Ingredients

1 cup whole pecans

zipper baggie

1 teaspoon vinegar

wooden spoon

3 egg whites

tape

pinch salt

Bible

1 cup sugar

. . . .

Preheat oven to 300° (do this first—very important)
Place pecans in zipper baggie and let children beat them with the wooden spoon to break into small pieces.

Explain that after Jesus was arrested, He was beaten by the Roman Soldiers. Read John 19: 1–3.

Let each child smell the vinegar. Put 1 teaspoon vinegar into mixing bowl.

Explain that when Jesus was thirsty on the cross, he was given vinegar to drink. Read John 19: 28–30.

Add egg whites to vinegar. Eggs represent life.

Explain that Jesus gave his life to give us life. Read John 10:10–11.

Sprinkle a little salt into each child's hand.
Let them taste it and brush the rest into the bowl.

Explain that this represents the salty tears shed by Jesus' followers, and the bitterness of our own sin. Read Luke 23:27.

So far, the ingredients are not very appetizing. Add 1 cup sugar.

Explain that the sweetest part of the story is that Jesus died because He loves us. He wants us to know Him and belong to Him. Read Psalms 34:8 and John 3:16.

Beat with a mixer on high speed for 12 to 15 minutes until stiff peaks are formed.

Explain that the color white represents the purity in God's eyes of those whose sins have been cleansed by Jesus.
Read Isaiah 1:18 and John 3:1–3.

Fold in broken nuts.
Drop by teaspoons onto wax paper covered cookie sheet.

Explain that each mound represents the rocky tomb where Jesus' body was laid. Read Matthew 27: 57–60.

Put the cookie sheet in the oven, close the door and turn the oven OFF.
Give each child a piece of tape and seal the oven door.

Explain that Jesus' tomb was sealed. Read Matthew 27: 65–66.

Go to bed!

Explain that they may feel sad to leave the cookies in the oven over-night. Jesus' followers were in despair when the tomb was sealed. Read John 16:20 and 22.

On Easter Morning, open the oven and give everyone a cookie.

Notice the cracked surface and take a bite. The cookies are hollow! On the first Easter, Jesus' followers were amazed to find the tomb open and empty. Read Matthew 28: 1–9.

how to have a taffy pull

My dad found this recipe in a magazine before me or my sisters were born and brought it home to my mom. My mom used to come have a Taffy Pull at school with us. I've done this with Laci's class and with my kids. It is SO much fun!

Ingredients

1 ½ cup sugar

1 cup molasses

½ teaspoon salt

1 cup heavy cream

2 tablespoons Butter

½ teaspoon baking soda

1 teaspoon lemon extract

. . . .

Place first four ingredients into a skillet or fry pot. Bring to a boil, stirring constantly. Reduce heat to medium and continue boiling until it reaches 265° F on a candy thermometer or until a small amount when dropped into cold water forms a firm ball (about 14 minutes). Remove from heat. Add butter, sprinkle with baking soda and lemon extract. Stir thoroughly. Pour onto large buttered platter. Cool 5 minutes. Turn edges into center. Continue cooling until cool enough to handle. Grease hands with butter. Cut taffy into 4 pieces. Roll into balls. Stretch and fold back and squeeze taffy into a lump. Repeat pulling, folding, and squeezing, incorporating air until it turns from brown to a golden amber. Pull taffy into long strips about ¾ inches in diameter and cut into 1 ½ inch pieces. Wrap in waxed paper and store in a closed tin. This is a wonderful recipe to take to school to do for your children's classmates.

cobblers, cakes & pies

cobbler

Ingredients

½ cup butter

1 cup self rising flour

1 cup milk

1 cup sugar

2 cups peaches or blueberries

*you may also mix 1 cup of blueberries and 1 cup of peaches for a different burst of flavor.

. . . .

Put butter in a 9 x 13 pan and place in 350 degree oven to melt butter.

Mix flour, milk and sugar while butter is melting.

Pour batter over butter. Spoon fruit over batter. DO NOT STIR.

Bake for 30–35 minutes.

pumpkin crisp

This recipe was given to me by my dearest friend Jennie Armstrong.
It quickly became a holiday favorite!

Ingredients

1 15 oz can pumpkin
1 cup evaporated milk
1 cup sugar
1 teaspoon vanilla extract
½ teaspoon ground cinnamon
1 box yellow butter cake mix
1 cup chopped pecans
1 cup melted butter
whipped cream
ground nutmeg

. . . .

Stir together first 5 ingredients. Pour into greased 9 x 13 baking dish.
Sprinkle cake mix over, sprinkle with pecans and drizzle with butter.
Bake at 350° for about an hour.
Serve with whipped cream and nutmeg.

peach or blueberry crisp

Ingredients

4 cups peaches or blueberries
½ cup all purpose flour
¾ cup oats
½ cup packed brown sugar
1 teaspoon cinnamon
½ cup butter

. . . .

Place fruit in 9 x 13 baking dish. Combine flour, oats, sugar and cinnamon. Cut in butter. Press over fruit to cover.

Bake at 325° for 30 to 35 minutes.

easy cookie dessert

Ingredients

1 package chocolate chip cookies
1 cup milk
1 tub Cool Whip

. . . .

Briefly dip cookies individually in milk and layer in 9 x 13 casserole dish. Top with a layer of cool whip. Repeat. Chill until ready to serve.

cheesecake banana pudding

My friend Liane brought this treasure to a Super Bowl party. She left the rest with us. I almost cried when I got to the last bite because it was SO good.

Ingredients

3 (8oz) blocks cream cheese

1 (14 oz) can sweetened condensed milk

1 (5.1oz) package instant vanilla pudding

2 cups milk

1 teaspoon vanilla

1 8oz cool whip

4 large bananas

1 12 oz package vanilla wafers

. . . .

Beat cream cheese and condensed milk 2 minutes. Beat pudding mix and milk with an electric mixer for 2 minutes. Add vanilla. Add to Cream Cheese mixture and beat 1 minute. Fold in whipped topping. Spoon 1/3 of the mixture into a 4 quart bowl. Top with 1/3 of bananas and wafers. Repeat twice, topping with wafers around the sides of the bowl. Chill 6 hours before serving.

lemon pie

Ingredients

1 small (3 oz) can of frozen lemonade, thawed (you can use lime)

1 can sweetened condensed milk

1 tub cool whip, thawed

1 graham cracker pie crust

. . . .

*M*ix lemonade, sweetened condensed milk and cool whip with electric mixer until fully blended. Pour into pie crust and chill.

chocolate pie

This recipe is from our good friend Kelly Coleman Call. I think she calls it Chocolate Sin pie. Yes, it's that good!

6 chocolate bars (with or without almonds)
1 (12 oz) tub of cool whip
1 prepared Chocolate pie crust

. . . .

*M*elt chocolate bars in the microwave in a large bowl. Stir in cool whip. Pour into pie crust and chill. This is also delicious with a layer of cream cheese between crust and filling.

176   E L I Z A B E T H   O.   S T E E D L E Y

little pecan pies

This recipe comes from my Aunt Nannie. We love these little pies, especially at the holidays.

Ingredients

1 stick butter, melted

1 cup sugar

2 eggs

1 teaspoon vanilla

1 teaspoon vinegar

1 cup finely chopped pecans

small ready to bake pie crusts

. . . .

*M*ix above ingredients. Brush pie crusts with crisco and prick with a fork. Spoon mixture into pie crusts and bake in 325 degree oven for 1 hour.

rose's coconut pie

This recipe is from my mother-in-law, Elizabeth. This pie will make its own crust.

Ingredients

4 eggs, well beaten
½ cup self rising flour
1 ¾ cup sugar
1 teaspoon vanilla
2 cups buttermilk
1 package of coconut

. . . .

*P*reheat oven to 325. Mix all ingredients and pour into 2 nine inch glass pie plates. Bake for 30 minutes.

it's a miracle pie

This recipe comes from my Aunt Nanny. It makes its own crust.

Ingredients

2 **cups milk**

4 **eggs**

1 ½ **cup sugar**

½ **cup flour**

1 **teaspoon vanilla**

¼ **cup butter**

. . . .

Combine milk, eggs, sugar and flour in a blender.

Stir in coconut, sherry and almonds to taste.

Bake in 8 inch pie plate at 350° for 40 minutes.

apple streusel pie

Several weeks ago, Heyward came home from school with a huge basket of apples. She said that all of the kids in her class gave them to her at lunch. She told them she would take them home and make apple pies. We had a wonderful time baking those pies.

Ingredients

1 deep dish ready made pie crust

3 cups peeled and sliced apples

¾ cup sugar

1 teaspoon cinnamon

¼ cup butter

½ cup brown sugar

1/3 cup all purpose flour

. . . .

Mix apples with cinnamon and sugar. Spoon into pie crust.

Mix butter, brown sugar and flour. Sprinkle over apples.

Bake at 425° for 15 minutes. Reduce temperature to 350 and bake for

35–45 minutes more until apples are tender.

new york cheesecake

This is the best classic cheesecake recipe I have found. I like it plain with no toppings.

Ingredients

1 cup graham cracker crumbs

3 tablespoons sugar

3 tablespoons melted butter

5–8 oz packages of Cream Cheese

1 cup sugar

3 tablespoons flour

1 tablespoons vanilla

1 cup Sour Cream

4 eggs

1 can cherry pie filling (optional)

. . . .

Mix crumbs, 3 tablespoons sugar and butter, press firmly onto bottom of 9 inch spring form pan. Bake at 325 for 10 minutes. Mix cream cheese, 1 cup sugar, flour and vanilla with electric mixer on medium speed until well blended. Add sour cream, mix well. Add eggs, one at a time, mixing on low after each addition until just blended. Pour over crust. Bake at 325 for 1 hour 10 minutes until center is almost set. Run knife or metal spatula around rim of pan to loosen. Cool before removing rim of pan. Refrigerate 4 hours or overnight. Top with pie filling (if desired) before serving.

black bottom cheesecake

Ingredients

Crust:

1 ¾ cups crushed Oreo cookies

1 tablespoon butter, melted

Filling:

3 bars Nestle Toll House premier white baking bars, broken into pieces

3 (8 oz) packages of cream cheese, softened

¾ cup granulated sugar,

2 teaspoon vanilla extract

3 large eggs

. . . .

Preheat oven to 350 Toss cookie crumbs and butter together in medium bowl. Press onto bottom of ungreased 9 inch spring form pan. Bake for 10 minutes. Microwave baking bars in medium bowl on 70% power for 1 minute. Stir. Microwave at additional 10–20 second intervals, stirring until smooth. Cool to room temperature. Beat cream cheese, sugar and vanilla in large mixer until smooth. Beat in eggs. Gradually beat in melted white baking bars. Spread over chocolate crust. Bake for 40 to 50 minutes or until edges are set but center still moves slightly. Cool in pan on wire rack. Refrigerate until firm.

Sprinkle with grated semi-sweet chocolate before serving.

brownie bottom cheesecake

Ingredients

1 package brownies

3 (8 oz) blocks cream cheese

¾ cup sugar

3 eggs

1 teaspoon vanilla

½ cup Sour Cream

. . . .

*M*ix brownies according to package directions. Bake in spring form pan at 325° for 35 minutes. Mix cream cheese cup sugar and vanilla with electric mixer on medium speed until well blended. Add eggs, 1 at a time, mixing on low speed after each addition just until blended. Blend in sour cream; pour over brownie bottom. Bake at 325° for 55 to 60 minutes or until center is almost set. Run knife or metal spatula around rim of pan to loosen cake; cool before removing rim of pan. Refrigerate 4 hours or overnight.

chocolate cake

I found this recipe in a magazine when I was in High School. It is
so moist and delicious!

Ingredients

1 ¾ cups all purpose flour

2 cups sugar

¾ cup powdered Cocoa

1 ½ teaspoons baking soda

1 ½ teaspoons baking powder

1 teaspoon salt

2 eggs

1 cup milk

½ cup vegetable oil

2 teaspoons vanilla extract

1 cup boiling water

. . . .

Mix dry ingredients in large mixing bowl. Add eggs, milk, oil and
vanilla. Beat 2 minutes at medium speed. Stir in boiling water (mixture will be thin). Pour into lined muffin tins (¾ full). Bake at 350°
for 18–20 minutes. Use knife test. Or pour into 3 greased rounds and
bake at 350° for 35–40 minutes. Frost with your choice of frosting.

cream cheese frosting

Ingredients

1 stick butter, softened

1 (8 oz) block cream cheese

1 teaspoon vanilla extract

1 16 oz box powdered sugar

. . . .

Cream butter and cream cheese. Add vanilla. Slowly beat in powdered sugar. Will ice 24 cupcakes or 1 cake.

chocolate cream cheese frosting

Ingredients

1 stick butter, softened

1 (8oz) block cream cheese

1 teaspoon vanilla extract

¼ cup Cocoa Powder

1 (16 oz) box powdered sugar

. . . .

Cream butter and cream cheese. Add vanilla. Slowly beat in cocoa powder and powdered sugar.

german chocolate icing

Ingredients

3 egg yolks

1 stick butter

1 cup sugar

1 cup cream

1 can of coconut

1 teaspoon vanilla

1 cup pecans

. . . .

Mix egg yolks, butter, cream and sugar. Bring to a boil over low heat. After it boils, add coconut, vanilla and nuts. Spread over cooled cake.

easy caramel cake

This recipe comes from good family friend Anne Thomas. I usually bake half sized layers (making 6 thinner layers) and double the icing recipe.

Ingredients

1 box butter recipe cake mix.
1 teaspoon vanilla
4 eggs instead of three

• • • • • • • • • • • • • • • • • • •

Mix and bake according to box directions. If making half layers, cut baking time to 10–12 minutes per layer

caramel icing

Ingredients

½ cup dark brown sugar

½ cup light brown sugar

1/3 cup carnation evaporated milk

1 stick plus almost another ½ stick butter

3 cups SIFTED powdered sugar

1 teaspoon vanilla

. . . .

*B*ring first 4 ingredients to a boil stirring constantly. When it boils beat in powdered sugar and vanilla. Ice cake immediately.

key lime cake

My mother-in-law, Elizabeth, introduced this cake to me. It is so delicious and makes quite a statement for something so easy.

Ingredients

1 package lemon cake mix

½ cup water

½ cup Key lime Juice

Zest of 2 Key limes

1 package lime gelatin

½ cup oil

4 eggs

. . . .

Mix all ingredients until just blended. Beat on medium speed 2 minutes. Pour into 3 greased cake pans. Bake at 350° for 25 minutes or until a toothpick inserted comes out clean. Ice with cream cheese frosting and garnish with additional key limes.

poppy seed cake

My Aunt Rachael has made this cake for as long as I can remember. It is a family favorite.

Ingredients

1 package yellow cake mix
1 package instant lemon OR vanilla pudding
4 eggs
½ cup sour cream
½ cup oil
½ cup sherry
½ cup sugar
¼ cup poppy seeds

. . . .

Mix all ingredients and beat on medium speed 2 minutes. Pour into greased bundt pan and bake at 350° for 50 minutes.

better than sex cake

Well ... it's not THAT good, but good none the less. It is a low fat recipe.

Ingredients

1 box German Choc Cake Mix–any brand

2 egg whites

10 oz. diet cola

1 jar caramel topping (ice cream topping)

8 oz. fat free whipped topping

Chocolate covered toffee candy bar–chopped into bits and pieces (1–¼ Cup)

. . . .

Spray 9x13 pan with Pam spray Chop toffee candy bar into small pieces (I put into a zippered sandwich bag and put that into another zippered sandwich bag and smash up with a measuring cup).

Mix together dry cake mix with egg whites and diet coke (do not use ingredients listed on cake box), until thoroughly blended. Mix in ½ cup chopped chocolate covered toffee bar candy. Pour into prepared pan.

Bake according to cake mix directions for 9x13 pan

When cake is done, poke holes in the cake with end of wooden spoon, or similar shaped object. Pour caramel topping into holes, letting caramel seep down and fill holes again. Do this a couple of times and pour rest of caramel across top of cake, spreading to cover cake as necessary. Sprinkle ½ cup chopped chocolate covered toffee bar on top of caramel. Spread whipped topping on cake. Sprinkle remaining ¼ Cup chopped chocolate covered toffee bar on whipped topping.

Keep refrigerated until serving.

conversation starters
.... *for* *table talk time*

Family time spent around the table is one of the Sweetest Blessings life can bring. It is a time for sharing our families hopes and dreams, building character in our children and learning about our children as well as teaching them about our lives and beliefs.

I e-mailed family and friends and asked them to send me questions that would encourage positive conversation at the dinner table. This is a sampling of questions that can be used. Please use these as a starting point for discussion at mealtimes. Most importantly, listen to the answers of your family members.

. . . .

What dreams or wishes didn't come true for you?

If you could do ONE thing over, what would that be?

As a child, what did you want to be when you grew up?

Where would you like to go on vacation if you could go anywhere in the world and why?

Who is your favorite character in the Bible and why?

What was your favorite Bible story when you were little?

If you were a vegetable what vegetable would you be and why?
Mom and Dad, tell your kids what your first date was like.

How did you meet? Did your parents like your boyfriend/ girlfriend? How did you propose?

What was your wedding like?

What (outdoor) games did you play when you were a child?

What was your favorite board game as a child?

What was your favorite book when you were young and why?

What does your mom or dad or grandmother cook that makes you feel special?

If you could start a charity, what kind would it be and why?

If you could have a superhero power, what would it be and why? And what would you call yourself?

What is your fondest memory of an outing with your mom, dad, or both?

What was your most tender day as a child?

What was your favorite Family Vacation and why?

What was your favorite Christmas and why?
What was your best school memory and why?

What was your favorite beach memory and why?

If you could go anywhere in the world, where would you go and how would you get there? plane, boat, car, train?

If you could spend 1 hour with any person (living or not), who would it be and why would you want to spend that time with them?

What one gift is your most prized possession and why?

If money was no object and you could give one gift to each member of your immediate family what would it be and why?

What is your favorite childhood fairy tale and why?

What is the one book you would read over and over?

If you could spend time with one famous chef, who would it be and what would you want them to teach you to cook?

Who is your favorite artist and why?

What dream would you like to accomplish in the next 6 months? What would you need to do to make that dream a reality?

Who did you help feel especially good about themselves today? How did you help them feel good?

Who did you make feel bad today? How could you have helped them feel good instead?

Who did you help in a special way today and how?

What did you say to your teacher today that was helpful or kind or something that made her feel good?

If you owned a pet motel where people could board their pets while they went away for a few days would you accept cats and dogs? Would you take a real small pony? What about a snake (non poisonous, of course)? A bird, a hamster? A squirrel?

What would you do if a squirrel got loose in the house?

If you found a tiny baby squirrel do you think you could get a Mother cat to nurse and take care of it?

index